Gross History

# Gross
## FACTS About
# the Roman Empire

BY MIRA VONNE

Raintree is an imprint of Capstone Global Library Limited, a company incorporated in England and Wales having its registered office at 264 Banbury Road, Oxford, OX2 7DY – Registered company number: 6695582

www.raintree.co.uk
myorders@raintree.co.uk

Edited by Mandy Robbins
Designed by Philippa Jenkins
Picture research by Wanda Winch
Production by Steve Walker
Printed and bound in China.

ISBN  978 1 4747 5216 9
21  20  19  18  17
10 9 8 7 6 5 4 3 2 1

British Library Cataloguing in Publication Data
A full catalogue record for this book is available from the British Library.

Photo Credits
Alamy: Lanmas, 5 (top); Bridgeman Images: © Look and Learn/Private Collection/Severino Baraldi, 25, © Bonhams, London, UK/Private Collection/Modesto Faustini, 7, © Historic England/ Private Collection/Judith Dobie, 9, Archives Charmet/Bibliotheque des Arts Decoratifs, Paris, France/Antonio Niccolini, 23, Archives Charmet/Private Collection/Italian School, 18-19, J. Paul Getty Museum, Los Angeles, USA/Roberto Bompiani, 17; Capstone, 5 (map); Getty Images: DEA Picture Library, 13; Johnny Shumate, 29; Newscom: akg-images/Peter Connolly, 11; North Wind Picture Archives, 15, Gerry Embleton, 21; Shutterstock: irin-k, fly design, Milan M, color splotch design, monkeystock, grunge drip design, Protasov AN, weevil, lice, parasites, Spectral-Design, 28; SuperStock: iberphoto, 27; Thinkstock: Photos.com, cover

Every effort has been made to contact copyright holders of material reproduced in this book. Any omissions will be rectified in subsequent printings if notice is given to the publisher.

All the internet addresses (URLs) given in this book were valid at the time of going to press. However, due to the dynamic nature of the internet, some addresses may have changed, or sites may have changed or ceased to exist since publication. While the author and publisher regret any inconvenience this may cause readers, no responsibility for any such changes can be accepted by either the author or the publisher.

# CONTENTS

# Filthy streets

The Roman **Empire** once ruled all the lands around the Mediterranean Sea. **Ancient** Romans had many tools that helped make their lives easier. But other parts of Roman life were dirty, gross or even deadly.

**empire**  large area ruled by a powerful leader

**ancient**  belonging to the very distant past and no longer in existence

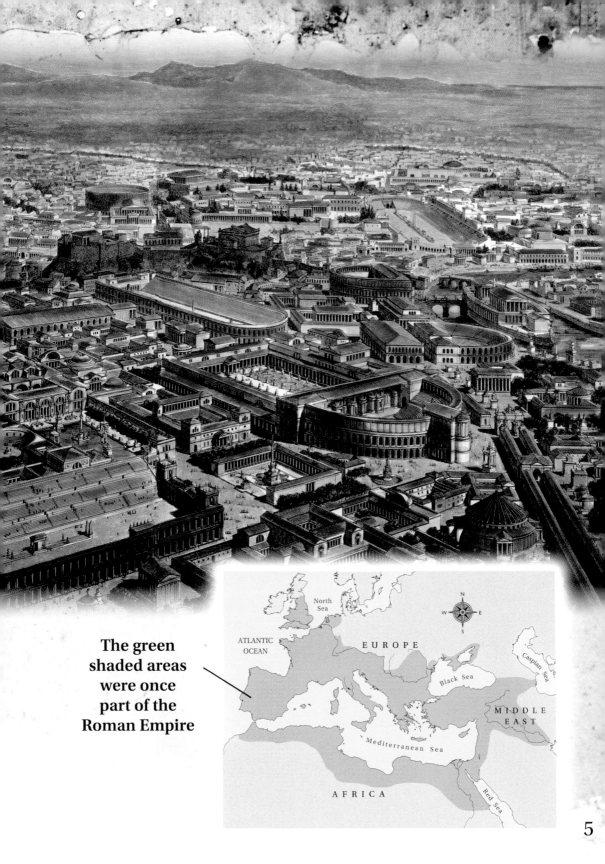

The green shaded areas were once part of the Roman Empire

ATLANTIC OCEAN

North Sea

EUROPE

Black Sea

Caspian Sea

MIDDLE EAST

Mediterranean Sea

AFRICA

Red Sea

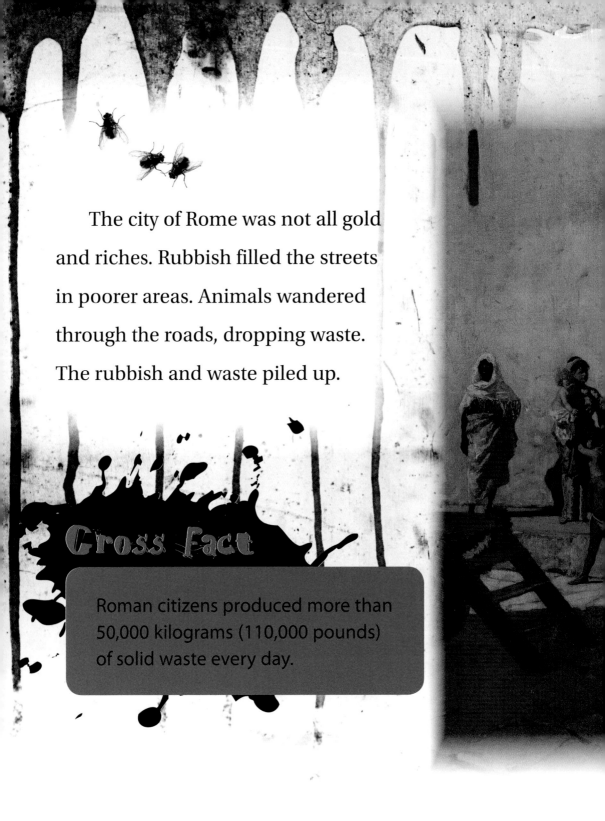

The city of Rome was not all gold and riches. Rubbish filled the streets in poorer areas. Animals wandered through the roads, dropping waste. The rubbish and waste piled up.

## Gross Fact

Roman citizens produced more than 50,000 kilograms (110,000 pounds) of solid waste every day.

Animals were **butchered** in the street for their meat. The remains were tossed into the sewer. Rainwater washed the waste from the sewers into the River Tiber. The awful smell of rotting flesh stayed behind.

**butcher**  cut up raw meat

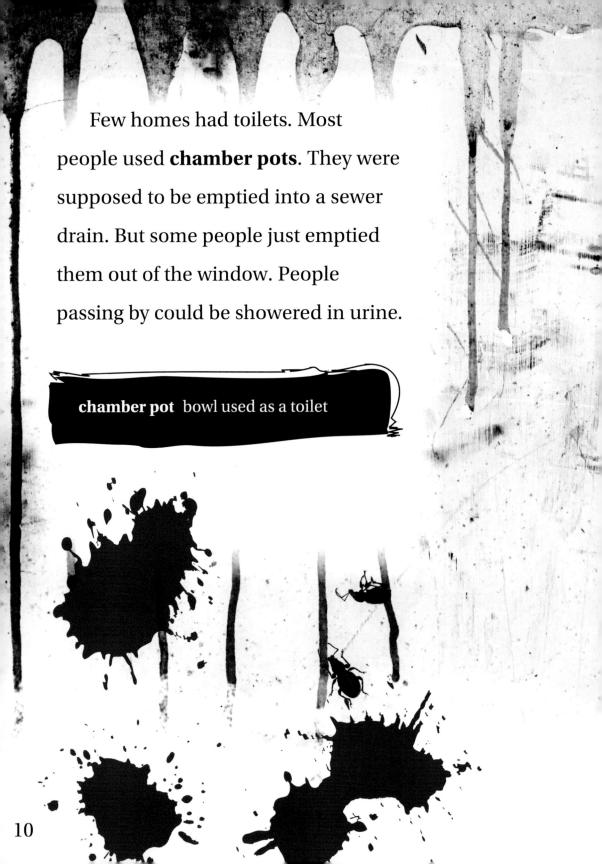

Few homes had toilets. Most people used **chamber pots**. They were supposed to be emptied into a sewer drain. But some people just emptied them out of the window. People passing by could be showered in urine.

**chamber pot** bowl used as a toilet

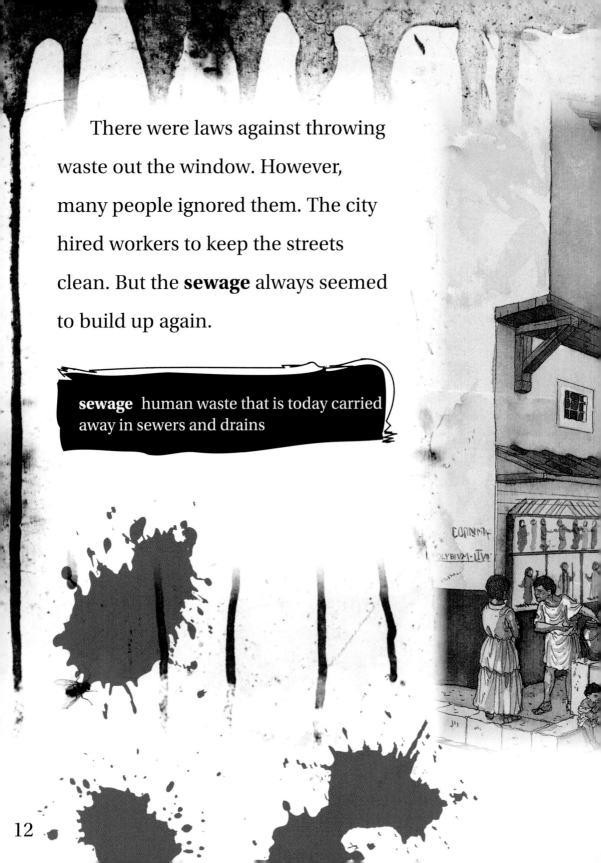

There were laws against throwing waste out the window. However, many people ignored them. The city hired workers to keep the streets clean. But the **sewage** always seemed to build up again.

**sewage** human waste that is today carried away in sewers and drains

# Citizens and slaves

Wealthy Romans bought and sold goods throughout the empire. This included people. For many enslaved people, life was horrible. Some owners **branded** or tattooed their slaves' faces. Others were bound with heavy chains.

**brand** mark the skin with a hot iron, sometimes as a mark of disgrace

Some enslaved people killed their babies at birth rather than let them become slaves.

# Gross grub

Rich Romans threw fancy dinner parties. Hosts served strange food such as tongue and brains. Sometimes birds were stuffed with mice. Guests ate all parts of the bird except its beak.

## Gross Fact

Cooking with garum was a popular practice. This sauce was made from aged fish heads, fins and guts.

# Keeping clean

Romans didn't have soap to wash clothes. Instead, laundry workers set out pots on the street. Roman men would relieve themselves into these pots. Dirty clothes were then soaked and scrubbed in huge tubs of urine.

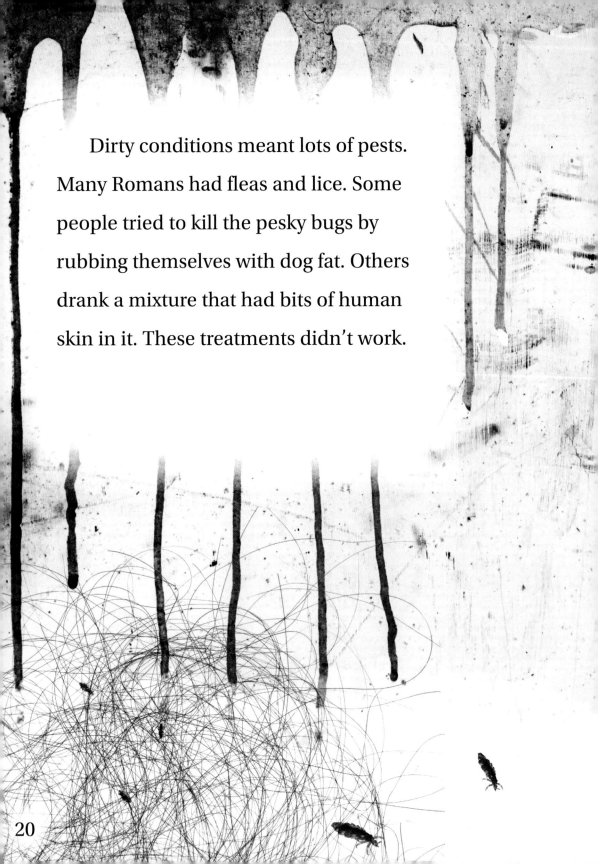

Dirty conditions meant lots of pests. Many Romans had fleas and lice. Some people tried to kill the pesky bugs by rubbing themselves with dog fat. Others drank a mixture that had bits of human skin in it. These treatments didn't work.

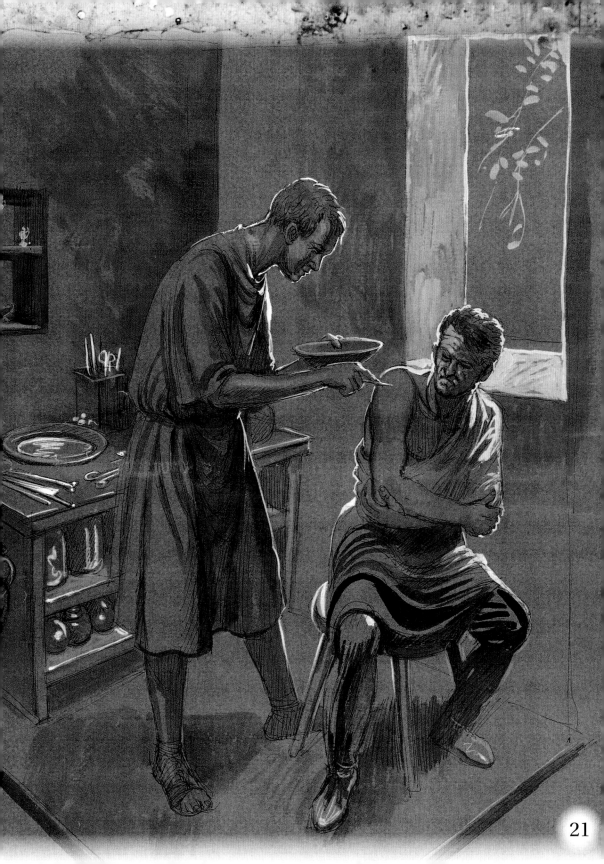

# Deadly sports

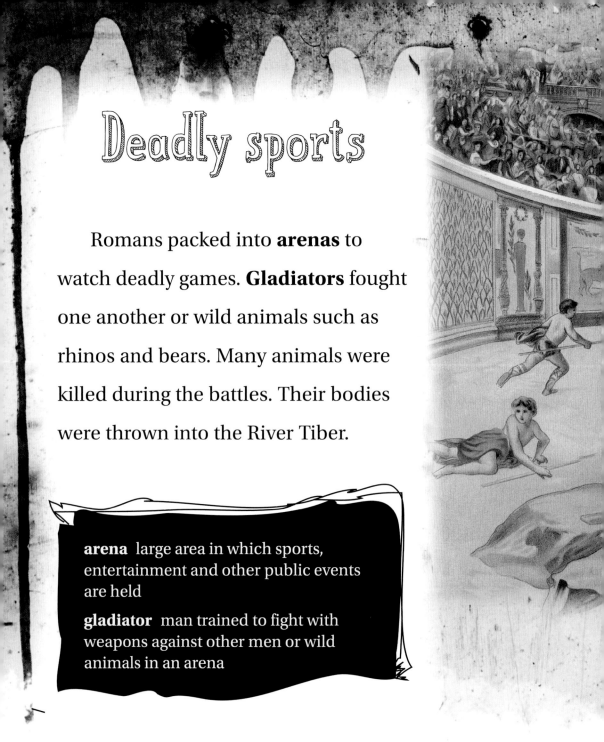

Romans packed into **arenas** to watch deadly games. **Gladiators** fought one another or wild animals such as rhinos and bears. Many animals were killed during the battles. Their bodies were thrown into the River Tiber.

**arena**  large area in which sports, entertainment and other public events are held

**gladiator**  man trained to fight with weapons against other men or wild animals in an arena

## Gross Fact

Being a gladiator wasn't all bad. Fighters ate three full meals a day and had medical care. If they lived long enough, they might even win their freedom.

Romans took their bloody games to the racetrack too. **Chariots** pulled by horses sped around the track. Sharp turns caused crashes. Drivers could be dragged to their deaths or crushed under hooves or wheels.

**chariot** two-wheeled horse-drawn vehicle used in ancient warfare and racing

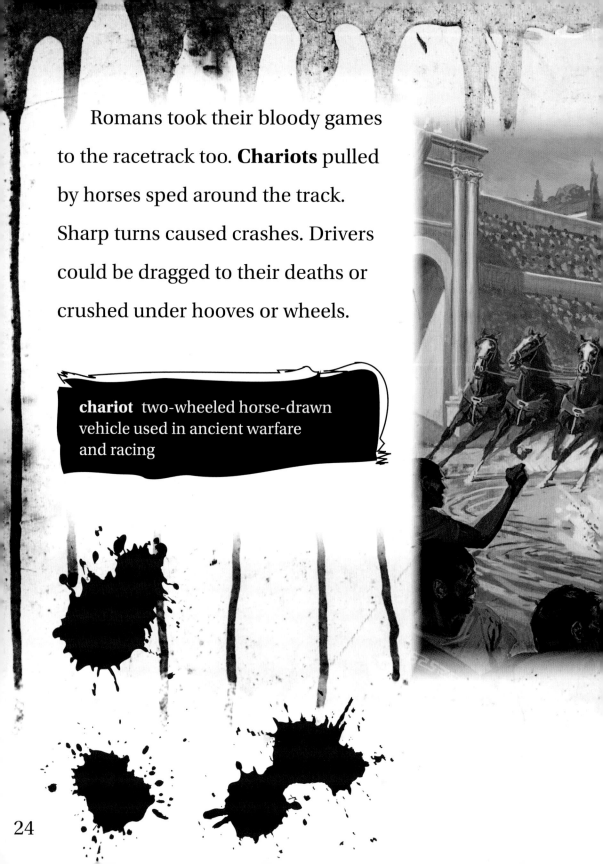

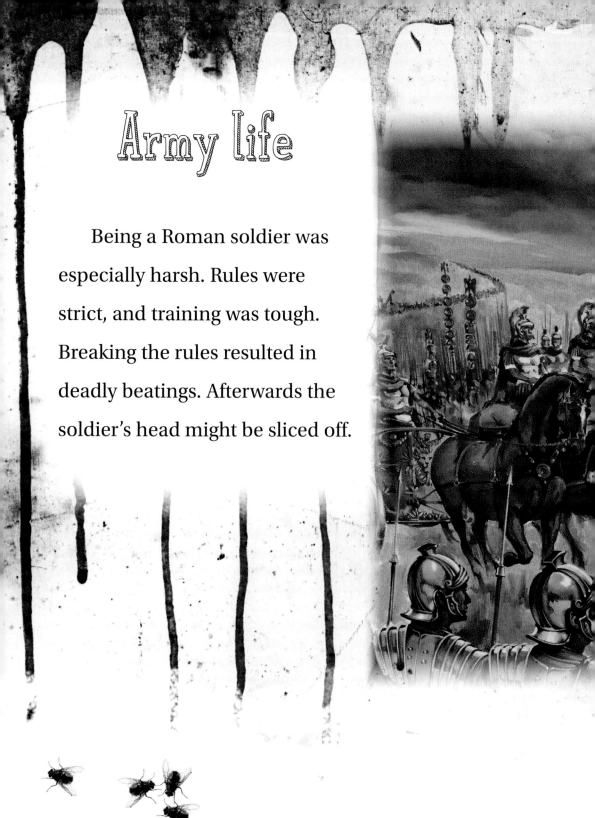

# Army life

Being a Roman soldier was especially harsh. Rules were strict, and training was tough. Breaking the rules resulted in deadly beatings. Afterwards the soldier's head might be sliced off.

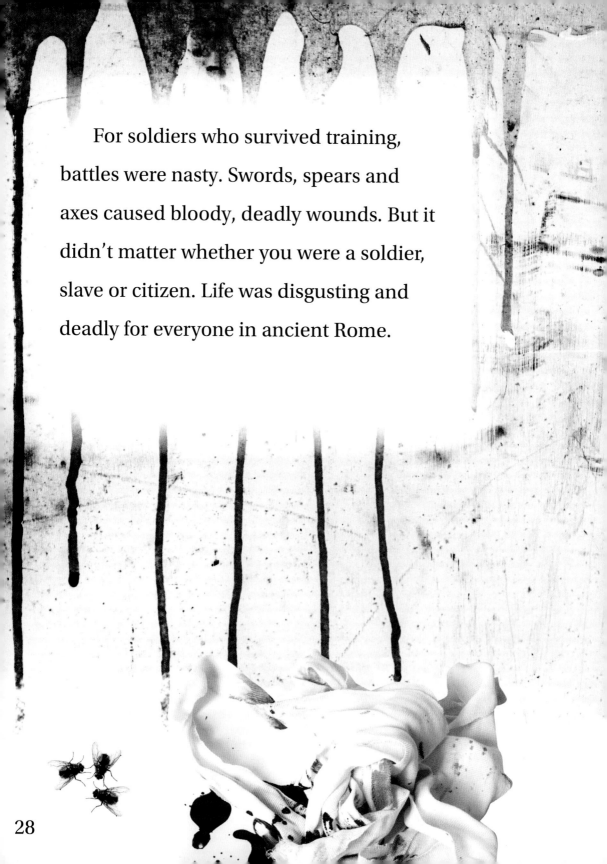

For soldiers who survived training, battles were nasty. Swords, spears and axes caused bloody, deadly wounds. But it didn't matter whether you were a soldier, slave or citizen. Life was disgusting and deadly for everyone in ancient Rome.

SHUMATE
2008

# Glossary

**ancient**  belonging to the very distant past and no longer in existence

**arena**  large area in which sports, entertainment and other public events are held

**brand**  mark the skin with a hot iron, sometimes as a mark of disgrace

**butcher**  cut up raw meat

**chamber pot**  bowl used as a toilet

**chariot**  two-wheeled horse-drawn vehicle used in ancient warfare and racing

**empire**  large area ruled by a powerful leader

**gladiator**  man trained to fight with weapons against other men or wild animals in an arena

**sewage**  human waste that is today carried away in sewers and drains

**sewer**  underground pipe for carrying off drainage water and waste matter

# Read more

*Romans* (Explore!), Jane Bingham (Wayland, 2017)

*Rotten Romans* (Horrible Histories), Terry Deary (Scholastic, 2016).

*You Wouldn't Want to Be a Roman Soldier*, David Stewart (Book House, 2016)

# Websites

**www.bbc.co.uk/education/topics/zwmpfg8**
Visit this website to find out what life was like in ancient Rome.

**www.ngkids.co.uk/history/10-facts-about-the-ancient-Romans**
Discover ten facts about the ancient Romans on this website from National Geographic Kids.

**www.dkfindout.com/uk/history/ancient-rome/**
This website has information about gladiators and the Roman army, among other topics.

# Comprehension questions

- The details in this book are gross. What other words can you use to describe the Roman Empire?

- How do the images add information about the Roman Empire? Describe some of these images.

- Consider how people lived in the Roman Empire. Would you want to live during this time? Why or why not?

# Index